# SCOTTISH SWEARING

Deedee Cuddihy

First Published 2020
Copyright©2020 by Deedee Cuddihy

No part of this book may be
reproduced, except for short extracts
for quotation or review, without the
written permission of the publisher
(unless it's the bits that I borrowed
myself, of course . . .)

ISBN 978 0 9930986 6 6

Published by Deedee Cuddihy
10 Otago Street,
Glasgow G12 8JH
Scotland

Cover design, graphics assistance and
research: Anonymous (Glasgow) Ltd.


Printed in Great Britain
by Bell and Bain Ltd, Glasgow

# Dedication

This book is dedicated to all those people whose (sweary) words I wrote down and used without them knowing it, and to those who willingly contributed, among them Pete Kirley, Jude Stewart, Madge Hashegan and Fiona Moore, not forgetting members of Pat Woods' book group at Hillhead Library in Glasgow.

*And a special mention to the graffiti "artists" whose work can be seen in the pedestrian underpass at the Burns Shopping Mall in Kilmarnock.

# Foreword

When planning my research for "The Wee Guide to Scottish Swearing", the intention had been to use my treasured bus pass to go on day trips from my home in Glasgow to various large towns and cities, there to spy on the local citizenry and jot down (surreptitiously!) their sweary utterances. (In fact, I already had a handful of such in a variety of notebooks going back several years.) But I had hardly got started when Covid-19 reared its ugly head. And so I had to confine the bulk of my research to areas of Glasgow that I could reach on foot. Fortunately, there were rich pickings to be had, some of it with a "lockdown" flavour. Friends provided content from areas of Scotland I couldn't reach and the internet threw up some additional sweary material. There are also contributions from people who come from outwith the UK but are now based here. Initially, I considered using asterisks for some words, particulary of the C variety but then I decided that cluttering the pages with ***** would detract from the humour and, dare I say it, the poetry of the content.

"Are you sayin' we're not married? Ye cheeky bastard - get tae fuck! And take a massive run aff a short, short pier!"

(Woman on a bus in Glasgow, shouting at her husband.)

# "Don't think aboot it - fuckin' dae it!"

(Woman to a man in Trongate. Glasgow.)

# "Get tae fuck, ye vultures!"

(homeless guy in Sauchiehall Street, Glasgow, scaring seagulls away while feeding Tunnocks caramel wafers and other biscuits to a flock of pigeons)

"No - I don't want tae see ma' balance! For fucksake - that's the last thing I want to look at."

(guy speaking to a cash machine in Sauchiehall Street, Glasgow)

"He says she wants to get married and she's no' even fuckin' pregnant? I says somethin's no' smellin' right here, son - get her tae fuck."

(man talking to a pal on Gt. George Street, off Byres Road in the West End of Glasgow)

# "I bumped into the wee man - he's fuckin' challenging me!"

(guy in Sauchiehall Street, Glasgow,
yellling to a pal)

"Yer no' watchin' where yer goin' . . . fucksake!"

(man in a wheelchair on Gt. Western Road, Glasgow being told off by his pal for steering it into a lamp post)

# "Ya fuckin' daftie!"

(one guy to another on a Glasgow bus
who, until that point, had been speaking
fluent Polish to each other)

# "Fuckin' nugget!"

(woman with kids, yelling at a man,
Glasgow city centre).

# "You'd better calm doon or I'm gonnae fuckin' bam you!"

(drunk guy in Partick, Glasgow talking to his even drunker pal)

I was like that: "Right,
you fuckin' bam!"
Know what I mean?

(guy talking to his girlfriend in
Sauchiehall Street, Glasgow)

"I *ken* who that is . . . Robert Downie Jr. - that's fuckin' Iron Man!"

(young guy on his phone in Central Station, low level, Glasgow)

# "I'll fuckin' roast you!"

(one angry bloke to another in Glasgow
city centre, overheard by John)

# "I'll take his wee face right aff, the wee fuck . . . he's no worth it!"

(woman in Sauchiehall Street on her phone)

# "Fuckin'
*ragin'* wi' me,
mate!"

(guy on a train from Glasgow to Airdrie,
talking about his boss to a colleague)

# "See Americans? Yer worse than the fuckin' English!"

(drunk bloke to the author on discovering she's American)

"It took me a long time to learn that the Scottish word for that thing you're wearing is a bum bag and not a fanny pack. Because in Scotland, fanny means pussy."

(American fire eater working on the Royal Mile in Edinburgh, calling out to a passerby)

# "Fucksake, big man - that must be the world's best fanny magnet!"

(young guy to Tom Brown. rickshaw operator in Glasgow city centre)

Commons authorities in Westminster have asked Scottish MPs to provide them with a list of Scottish swear words so they can improve politicians' online security. One Scottish MP said: "The request did give us a bit of a chuckle to begin with but there is a serious point to all of this."

(Torcuil Crichton writing in the Daily Record)

# "You Sassanach bastard!"

(very drunk man on his phone, failing to persuade a taxi driver to pick him up outside M&S in Argyle Street, Glasgow)

A man walks into a butcher's shop in Ayr where the butcher is standing behind the counter with his hands behind his back, and asks: *"Is that yer Ayrshire bacon?"* and the butcher replies: *"No, I'm just warming my hands."*

(old joke)

Just walked past a crowd leaving a panto in Glasgow. Not sure what they were talking about but...

**Lady**: *"oh no I'm not!"*
**Man**: *"aye ye f\*\*\*n are hen!"*

Both laughed.

(Calum Macdonald, BBC Radio Scotland presenter, tweeting in December, 2019)

A Scots movie is set for the record books before it's screened - for swearing. "One Day Removals" uses the F word more than 320 times, the most ever in a Scottish-made film. The stars, Patrick Wright and Scott Ironside, are removal men who end up with a vanload of bodies after a simple job goes horribly wrong. Director and writer Mark Stirton, 37, said: "I may actually cut the number of F words before it's released so people can just concentrate on the film."

(Bob Dow writing in the Daily Record)

TOP LEVEL SWEARING
Ex-Rangers ace David Robertson uses F-word 80 TIMES in new BBC Scotland documentary – and viewers love him for turning the airwaves blue.     The former Scotland defender, 50, swore an incredible 100 times during the hour-long show Real Kashmir FC.

(from The Sun)

**Officer**: *"So you're thinking of leaving us?"*
**Cammy**: *"Absofuckinglutely sir. I'm offski."*

(from the National Theatre of Scotland's play "Black Watch" by Gregory Burke)

*"Kiss ma sweaty balls, you fat fuck!"*

(Scottish actor, Peter Capaldi, playing
Malcolm Tucker in Scottish writer,
Armando Iannucci's "In the Loop")

# *"Patterson - ya fanny!"*

(young guy in a car shouting out to a pal walking on Dumbarton Road in Partick, Glasgow)

# "Open the door, you fuckin' wide-o!"

(young guy on Byres Road, Glasgow,
said jokingly to a pal who was giving
him a lift in his car)

# "Get it up you!"

(two guys in a car on Woodlands Road in Glasgow, shouting out to pedestrians)

# "I'll smash that cunt in, man . . . cheeky wee bastard."

(drunk guy in the street, Glasgow)

After the Kung Fu movies came out in the 1970s, a friend of mine started saying, as a joke, if someone was drunk: *"Is that Kung Fu?"* because "fu" is a Scottish word meaning drunk and Kung sounds like "cunt".

(Charlie)

The worst swearing I've ever heard was at a warehouse I worked in back in the 1960s, in Glasgow. During the week the guys weren't too bad but they'd come in on a Saturday morning, still drunk from the night before and they'd say things to each other like: *"I'll put you in hospital, you cunt!"* It never got physical but the level of verbal aggression was disturbing.

(Iain)

"Aye - she's a nice lassie but he's a cunt . . . the wide-o."

(one bloke to another bloke, Glasgow)

MHAIRI Black has become the first MP to say "c\*\*\*" in parliament - dropping the C-bomb FOUR times to highlight misogynistic abuse.

(from The Sun)

# "I seen it on YouTube - just a mad cunt in a hoose."

(young guy drinking Buckfast in a doorway with a group of pals in Union Street, Glasgow)

"Still a fuck-up of a dad in many ways - anything to do with emotions and he didn't want to know. "

(young guy in Sauchiehall Street, Glasgow talking to a friend)

"I went in for a normal handshake and he went in for a bro shake so I really fucked it up."

(young guy to another guy in Finnieston, Glasgow)

# "Look at these fucking cultural references all over the place!"

(young guy to another young guy in the West End of Glasgow)

". . . but, like, you need a fucking gallery to sell your work!"

(young woman speaking to two pals in the West End of Glasgow)

I took a couple of puffs and I thought "Oh my lord - I'm away with the fucking fairies now!"

(young woman on her phone to a pal, Glasgow)

"He's coming up to the flat and selling weed . . . All that shite is going to fuck up your mental health."

(one young guy to another, walking along Kelvin Way in Glasgow)

# "I'm not goin' in tae pure fuckin' "War n' Peace" - it is what it is!"

(young woman on her phone to a friend on the train)

Someone just told me
I look like Lawrence
Olivier. I thought:
*"Fucksake - he's
been dead for 30
years! Who's it going
to be next week -
King f*****'
Canute?"*

(Allan Tall)

"Yeah - they're all sitting around a fire singing songs - how fucking original!"

(three young guys talking on Byres Road, Glasgow)

"To get to the Greyhound station we had to go through probably the worst ghetto in LA so Murdo was shittin' himself!"

(young guy talking to another young guy on a bus)

**Maryhill's *not* a shite hole!**

Aye, it is.

**Well . . . it *might* be a shite hole - but it's better than Milngavie!"**

(two young guys having an argument in the street one night in the West End of Glasgow)

# "Fuck you, you fucking privileged cunt - I'm from Glasgow!"

(bloke shouting on Gt. Western Road in Glasgow one night)

# BAWBAG'S BACK!

Hurricane Bawbag which sparked travel chaos in 2011, could return to Scotland as experts warn the nation faces its stormiest autumn for years.

(The Sun, Sept. 2017)

# "Yer maw has baws and yer da loves it."

(Sarah)

# "If yer auntie had baws she'd be yer uncle."

(Rob Gibson in an email)

## THE WEE GUIDE TO
## SCOTTISH SWEARING

A Glasgow university lecturer will be turning the air blue later this month at a lunch time talk on the "Psychology of Swearing." Tickets for the X-rated free event at the university were snapped up within hours of being advertised on social media. Dr. Emily Nordmann who jokingly refers to herself on Twitter as "Dr. Swearypuss", has warned that the hour-long talk will contain: "frequent use of extremely offensive language." The academic has previously published an on-line article entitled "Five f***ing fascinating facts about swearing".

(from a news report)

Research has found that those with higher IQs tend to swear more. The study, published by the Language Sciences journal, also revealed that people who tend to swear more may in fact have a larger vocabulary than those who don't.

(from a report in the Glasgow Herald)

# "I'll fuckin' ragdoll you in a minute, ya' fuckin' ginger cow! An' I hope you fuckin' get corona virus, you cunt!"

(crazy woman at Partick bus station in Glasgow, shouting at a young woman she didn't know - and whose hair was only very slightly ginger)

*Ragdoll: To be forcefully grabbed and shaken with such ferocity that the recipient resembles a ragdoll.*

# "There's gonnae be a *situation* if you gie me a fuckin' warnin'!"

(angry drunk man to police officers who were trying to persuade him and his pal from drinking together in a boarded-up pub doorway in Glasgow during the lockdown)

# "Observe some fucking social distancing, you prick!"

(angry man at an artisan cheese shop in the West End of Glasgow, to the bloke standing behind him in the queue. *Thanks to Iain Scott*)

*"Just had a run in with 5 well dressed, teenage boys on Woodlands Rd who were hanging outside a shop and saw me approaching but would not move, staring me out.. l waited..l had bags of shopping and the road was busy so... l went Dundonian on their asses and called them a bunch of arrogant, middle-class wankers and told them to get out of my f#\*king space. Pricks."*

(Tulip on facebook during the lockdown)

# "We have a cure! No fuckin' vaccines here!"

(crazy guy in camoflage gear, on his bike in Sauchiehall Street, Glasgow, yelling at the top of his voice, during the lockdown)

"How can you ask them to come back to work? Fuck knows, mate. How are they going to fuckin' pay them? Fuckin' somethin' s' no' addin' up here, mate. He's tryin' tae pull the fuckin' wool over the council's eyes."

(guy in the Waitrose queue during the lockdown, taking a call from a work colleague)

**First man:** *"I see yer fadin' away tae fuck all with that walkin'.*

**Second man:** *"Do you think so? I've put on half-a-stone!"*

(two middle-aged guys greeting each other on the street in Hyndland, Glasgow during the lockdown)

# "Saves me interacting with cunts like you."

(cafe owner in the West End of Glasgow on why he was enjoying running his business as a takeaway during the lockdown.)

"I'm absolutely fuckin' up tae high doh! We're tryin' to deal with a pandemic and we've got people bending the rules!"

(Scottish comedian, Janey Godley's spoof subtitles on the speech made by First Minister, Nicola Sturgeon following the revelation that her chief medical officer had broken the lockdown rules)

"Hello Primary 7b and Parents/ Carers: It was brought to my attention that there had been some swearing during our quiz on Thursday. There were also some rude remarks made about some of the questions that members of our class were asking. After listening to a recording of the quiz, I am confident that I know who was responsible. This will not be tolerated and if it happens again, I won't make the effort it takes to continue with these sessions that so many of us have been enjoying."

(P7 teacher in Fife, writing on the school's website during the lockdown)

"In the classroom we learn to read and write but in the playground . . . we learn to swear."

(Cora Bissett, actor, director, playwright and musician, from Fife, in her BBC Scotland documentary about swearing: "Scotland - Contains Strong Language" broadcast on April 7, 2020)

FUCK
THY
NEIGHBOUR
Bros
778 5591

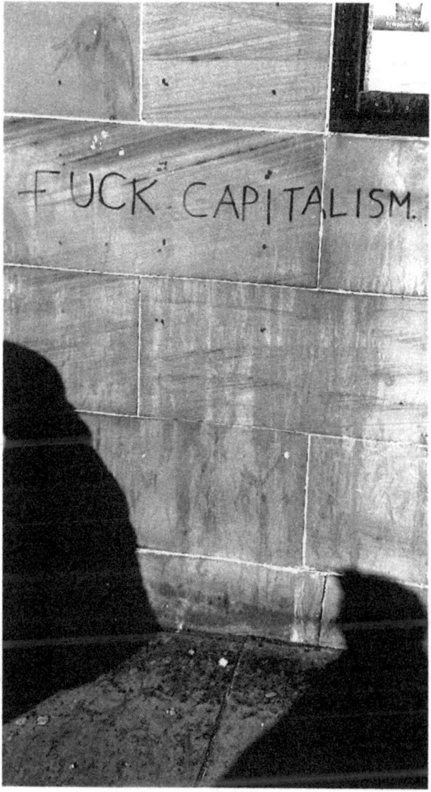
FUCK CAPITALISM.

NO MORE GE
OF SINGULARITY
upend the
totalizing notive
authority of modern
architectural history
BEAMS · COLUMNS · SLABS
FUCK PURISM
continual erasure
UTOPIAN WHOLES
UTOPIAN HOLES
MONOMANIA
a past more contingent
and less monolithic
NO MORE GENIUS
BULLSHIT
Property
and
self property
THE TYRANNY
OF SINGULARITY
MONOMANIA
HOLES

Ya limp
Buiscit
Greedy Cunt

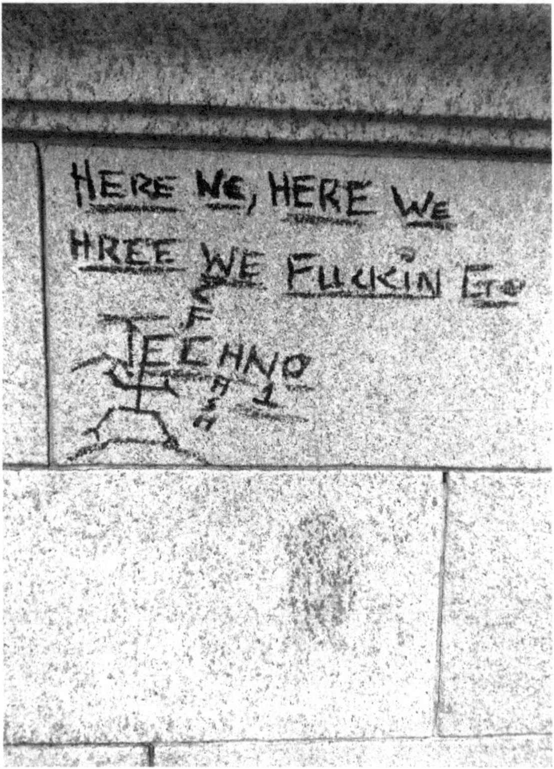
HERE WE, HERE WE
HREE WE FUCKIN
TECHNO

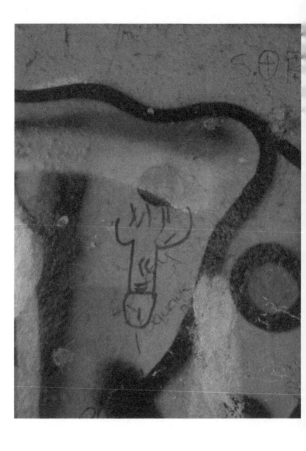

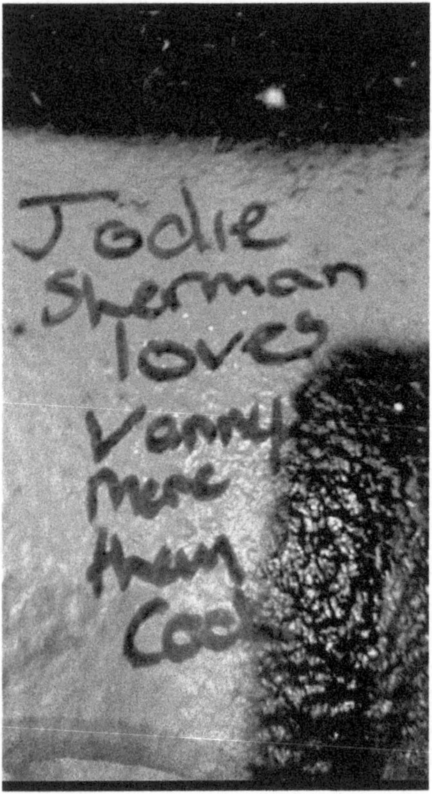
Jodie
Sherman
loves

# DICK
# INSTITUTE

GALLERY · MUSEUM · LIBRARY

| | |
|-----|-------------|
| MON | Closed |
| TUE | 11am-6pm |
| WED | 10am-8pm |
| THU | 1pm-8pm |
| FRI | 10am-4pm |
| SAT | 10am-4pm |
| SUN | Closed |

Level access at rear

Lift available

Assistance Dogs only

FREE
ENTRY

At the primary school I went to back in the late 1950s, the closest we got to swearing was shouting *"Aaaah . . . keech toley bum fart!"* to each other in the playground.

(Pete Kirley)

*"Eech meech hen's keech toley bum fart"* is one of the things we used to say in the primary school playground in Dundee.

(Madge)

If someone was crying in the playground, you'd hear kids chanting: *"Yer yer ma's big bubbly bairn!"* or *"She's her ma's big bubbly bairn!"* or *"He's his ma's big bubbly bairn!"* and if you saw a kid pick a sweetie up off the ground and eat it, the chant would be: *"Pickie aff the grund!"* because it was seen as a really disgusting thing to do.

(Annie, from Dundee)

We were from Manchester but we moved to a small town outside Edinburgh when I was nine and in the school playground one day I said *"bloody hell"* and one of the girls looked a bit shocked and said *"you swore!"* but I didn't know what she meant. This was in the 1950s and *"bloody hell"* was just an expression my father used a lot.

(Lis)

I was 15 or 16 - this was in the late 1950s - and a girl at school who was a bit older said *"hells bells and buckets of blood"* and I thought it was so sophisticated!

(Joyce)

We were from Dundee and it was well known in the area that my grannie had aspirations. She'd sent my mum and her sister to elocution lessons. I can remember playing outside with the other kids in the area when I was about three and one of them said to me: *"Yer grannie disnae let you swear!"* and I said: *"Yes she does - you currant!"* which was how I thought a bad word I'd heard was pronounced.

(Jude)

"We've never used the f word at home so I was very surprised one day when I heard my 3-year-old son out in the back garden, looking a bit distressed and saying: *"Fuck sake . . . where's my Noddy car?"*

(Carol)

I've always had a way with words. More specifically, swear words. At the tender age of six, sat in the back of the car with my family, I was several hours into a long journey when I threw down the book I was reading. Asked what was wrong, I announced matter-of-factly to the car: *"I can't see a word because of the f****** sun."* My grandparents looked horrified and my father, who knew exactly where I had picked up the new addition to my vocabulary, sheepishly drove on.

(Nicola Love, journalist, writing in the Glasgow Herald)

We used to say *"mammy, daddy"* when we were kids, if we'd hurt ourselves; and when we got older it was *"ya bastard!"* but not in front of our parents. I never swore in front of them even though my dad swore a lot.

(Marion)

My mother, if I swore, she'd hit me because we weren't allowed to swear. So I started saying *"shangalang"* which was a word I made up to use instead of swearing. Then my mother would say: *"What's that?"* and I'd tell her: *"I said shangalang."*

(The late Scottish song writer, Bill Martin, talking about "Shang-a-lang", the smash hit song he and Phil Coulter wrote for the Bay City Rollers.)

At school on the Isle of Skye in the 1960s and '70s, there was no swearing - not that I can remember; not from the kids or the teachers. People were very "churchy" then - Free Presbyterian - even if they didn't go to church themselves. Although, oddly enough, it wasn't unknown for quite respectacle members of the Gaelic-speaking community, women and men, to sprinkle their sentences with the occasional swear word including the Gaelic for "cunt" which was seen as nothing worse than "damn" is in English.

(Fiona)

I used to know a boy in Cleland who never swore literally (probably for religious reasons) but always substituted *"fucking"* with *" buckin' "* which he used for every second or third word in a sentence.

(Mathew, from a text)

We're from Bridgeton in the East End of Glasgow and to avoid actual swearing, my mum used to say: *"You're gettin' on my buckin' nerves!"*

(Bill)

My father used to say
*"yer arse an' parsley"*
if you said something
he didn't agree with.

(Alistair)

There wasn't a lot of swearing in our house when I was growing up in Dundee. My dad would say *"bloody"* and *"bloody buggering hell"* from time to time as well as *"jeezy peeps"* which I think was a Dundee variation on *"Jesus"*. And you'd say *"keech"* instead of *"shit"* or *"shite"*. In fact, there was a kind of poem about keech which was: *"The people they're funny in Brechin. They never say shittin', they always say keechin'."*

(Sandra)

*"I wouldn't marry him
if his arse was lined
with bloody silver!"*
That's what my
widowed granny said
when it was suggested
she marry her lodger
who seemed quite keen
on the idea.

(Les)

The first time I can remember hearing my mother swear was when she was 70. It was after my father had died and I came up from London to stay with her one weekend and heard her shout *"fuck!"* from the kitchen, due to some minor incident. It was very funny! But I was surprised because my parents didn't swear - certainly not in front of us. I think it was some kind of release for my mum and from then on I'd hear her say *"fuck"* from time to time when I was visiting - and she lived until her 100th year!

(Linda)

If I hear any sweary words in the house, I say: *"Language! Language!"*. We weren't a swearing household when I was growing up and I still don't swear. Although the first word my wee nephew said was *"shit"* which was something his mum realised she'd been saying a lot without being aware of it so she had to start saying *"sugar"* instead.

(Britt)

My parents didn't swear at home but I started swearing at secondary school and I've carried on ever since. *"Fuck"* and *"shit"* punctuate a lot of my sentences and not just when I'm angry. I don't swear at work and I've never sworn in front of my mum but I do swear when I'm out with my friends. My partner isn't very sweary and doesn't like me swearing at home especially now that we have a child. He's four and after I heard him say *"fuck"* a few times I stopped saying that at home. And I've substituted *"sugar"* for *"shit"* when I'm in the house. The sweariest my mum ever gets is *"Oh God"* which I've noticed my son saying a few times, after she's been looking after him, which is quite funny.

(Karen)

When I'm feeling homesick for Dundee I'll give my stepmum a call and ask her to swear down the phone for me. She'll say: *"Em gonnae punch your fuckin' pus!"* She's very Dundonian.

(Jasmine)

I was brought up in
Ireland and the closest
my mum came to
swearing was saying
*"God between and all
harm"* and *"Blessed
Ireland"*.

(Carol)

My mum would say *"Jesus fuckin' Christ almighty!"* when she was angry.

(Lydia)

I use the F word a lot at home but I'd never use the C word. But my daughters and their friends, who are in their 20s, use the C word all the time which I find really offensive.

(Louise)

A TEACHER struck off for a string of foul-mouthed comments to pupils in a North Ayrshire secondary school has claimed he's a victim of political correctness. The 54-year-old who had previously worked in the Australian prison service, called a pupil a "fat c***" and told another child "I've sh****d your mum". He's been banned from the classroom following a disciplinary hearing, despite glowing tributes from former pupils who said his "informality" helped make him an "inspirational" teacher.

(from a news report)

PUPILS should be allowed to swear in the classroom rather than be punished for their four-letter-word outbursts, according to the Scottish Parent Teacher Council. But a spokesperson for the Headteachers' Association of Scotland has said that swearing should not be tolerated in the classroom. However, he added: *"I do know of schools where teachers have learned to live with it because if they excluded all pupils who swore, there would be no one left."*

(from a news report)

I worked in a primary school in Parkhead, in the East End of Glasgow, where calling someone a cow was a huge insult. So you might hear a kid say: *"She called your ma a fucking c-o-w"*, spelling the word cow.

(Anne)

Is *"cow"* a bad thing to call someone in Scotland? I was in a taxi in Glasgow and a woman stepped out in front of it and the driver shouted out: *"You cow!"* but I didn't understand why he said that.

(Sunny, from Taiwan)

*"Tongs ya bass"*
is what the lads
said in the List D
school I worked
in years ago.

(Val)

If we were out in the street or on a bus or a train, and my mother heard someone saying *"Jesus"* in a sweary way, she'd confront them and say: *"Excuse me - you're talking about a friend of mine!"*

(the late Fay Duffy)

Further to our article headlined **'Breach of the Preach',** we would like to make it clear that the (lay preacher) convicted of careless driving near Fenwick, Ayrshire was not charged or convicted of swearing or using foul language. We apologise for any misunderstanding this may have caused.

(from a Scottish newspaper)

Scotland introduced swear words to the modern world, according to research. Anglo-Saxons invented many of our modern swear words but they went out of fashion until medieval Scots poets revived them to spice up their bawdy verses. The 16th century bards churned out shocking tales littered with taboo words at a time when swearing was thought to anger God. But they went down a treat with audiences and bad language became so popular in Scotland that the Blasphemy Act had to be passed in 1551.

(Kevin Hurley writing in the Daily Record)

A swearing parrot from Kilmarnock has become a huge internet hit. Videos of Sparky turning the air blue have racked up more than three million hits on YouTube. He squawks X-rated one-liners such as: "I'll boot yer b**s son", "haw b**bag" and "Aw for f***'s sake". But not everybody approves of the foul-mouthed bird, with one objector in America contacting the owners to tell them that: *"God is angry with the parrot who swears."*

(from a news story)

**Q. What is the oddest tattoo you have been asked to do?**

**A.** The words *"fuck the Christ"* beside a profile of the devil on the back of a guy's neck. Apparently it was something to do with a falling out he'd had with a priest. And he came in 15 - 20 years later to get it covered up.

(Johnny McNeillie, interviewed for the author's book "Under the Skin of the Scottish Tattoo")

"I note from your police interview that you said *'I've been an arsehole'*. I can only agree."

(Comment made by the late Sheriff Deirdre MacNeill when addressing the accused - who was found guilty - at court in Edinburgh; from her obituary in the Glasgow Herald, June 2020)

"Heh, see my first visit to see him in Greenock? Fuckin' finishin' ma fag and he says "Excuse me . . . " A fuckin' £50 fine on the spot! I had two weeks to pay!"

(man on a train talking about being fined for smoking outside Greenock prison when visiting a family member, after the smoking ban had been introduced)

"I didn't know I had to be in the f*****' court for half eleven! My drugs support worker never told me."

(Woman on a bus in Clydebank)

"You've been caught *'hoorin' around'*, to use the Perth vernacular."

(Stuart Cosgrove on BBC Radio Scotland's "Off the Ball", to a guest who had been contributing to lots of other radio and TV programmes)

The word *"hooer"* is popular here in Crieff, as verb and noun, e.g. *"It's a hooer of a day, is it no?"* and *"He's been hooering up and doon the high street a' day on his new motorbike."*

(Nathan in an email)

It was a hot day and I was waiting at a bus stop on the south side of Glasgow when a boy who couldn't have been more than 10-years-old and was with his parents, said to them: *"I'm sweatin' like a hoor."* It's not the sort of expression you expect a child to come out with but I guess it was something that was said in his family because neither his mum nor dad remarked on it. I'd never heard it before myself.

(Jane)

# *"I'm* the shite bag? *You're* the fuckin' shite bag!"

(One 30s guy to another 30s guy, Sauchiehall Street. sitting on a bench)

"Check out the Willie World News. I review the new tractors. They're all shite."

(Groundskeeper Willie in the Simpsons)

# "How are ye, ye big shite?"

(man boarding a bus, greeting a man already on it who then tells the other passengers: "It's okay, folks - he's ma wee brother!")

*"Did you fuckin' con me the last time?"*

*"No I didn't - you're talkin' shite!"*

(two guys in Sauchiehall Street, Glasgow)

My grannie, who was from Portsoy, on the Moray coast in Aberdeenshire, had some strange expressions one of which was: *"She speaks as the duck shites - and that's at random."* I was never sure what they meant or if she had made them up herself but they were great.

(Helen)

With a guilty guffaw, Avril tells a story that shows Kesson retained her aversion to bullshit to the end. "She was in hospital, very ill. She hadn't spoken for two weeks and my brother Kenny came in having had a good few drinks. It was a wild night, raining and everything else and he said: *'Mum, these are the tears of God, weeping for you.'* She sort of stirred, turned to him and said: *'Aw, shite, Kenny,'* and then she died. To think those were the last words of a fine writer, but it makes me laugh" she says.

(Jessie Kesson's daughter, Avril, interviewed by journalist Dani Garavelli in 2018)

The late Magnus Magnusson, journalist and TV presenter, told a story - to illustrate Scottish dialects - about an elderly woman getting on a bus in Aberdeenshire and, spotting an acquaintance with a baby girl in her arms, goes and sits beside her. Looking fondly at the wee one, she asks her: *"And can you talk yet?"* To which the baby replies: *"Awa' an' shite!"* Impressed, the old dear says to her friend: *"Whit a rare speaker!"*

(from a BBC Radio Scotland broadcast)

When I was growing up in Aberdeen in the 1960s, I remember seeing *"TOT LOVES FUD"* written on walls all over the place. It means *"cock loves fanny"*.

(Clare)

# " 'Cos I *ken* who she fuckin' is, ya fudd!"

(two young guys in Dumfries in the street)

" *'mon tae* " and *"get tae"* are two examples of the way, in Scotland, you can swear without using actual swear words, being shortened versions of *"come on tae fuck"* and *"get tae fuck"*.

(with thanks to the late John Samson who had a great way with words)

I moved to Glasgow from America back in the late 1970s and I can remember asking one of the people I'd become friendly with: "What is this expression *"get tae fuck"* that I keep hearing?"

(Maryann)

"Swearing used to be called *"industrial language"* because only people who worked in the ship yards used it."

(Joyce)

Swearing in Scotland is also known as *"agricultural language"* due to the fact that people who work on farms swear so much. It's just the way they're brought up.

(Rosemary)

My mother was from Shetland but she picked up some basic Gaelic - observations about the weather, terms of endearment and swearing - after she got married and moved to Skye. Later on, she worked in a tourist information office in the Highlands and whenever she had to deal with a particularly demanding customer, she'd conclude the conversation with a smile and a cheery: *"Thalla 's cac"* which they probably thought was *"Have a good day"* but was actually Gaelic for *"Away and shite."*

(Rowan)

The only person who swore in our house when I was growing up in Glasgow was my dad who used to say *"haramzada"* quite often when he was annoyed or angry about something. It's the Punjabi word for *"bastard"*.

(Nadia)

I say *"verdammt heilige scheisse"* when I don't want people to know that I'm swearing. It's German for *"fucking holy shit"* and I learned it from a German student we had staying with us back in the 1950s, when I was a teenager - although sometimes I just say *"scheisse"* instead of the full German.

(Marlene)

There is a Chinese word for *"bitch"* and we would use it, for instance, for a woman who is trying to steal your husband or she does something wrong. 100 per cent you would use that word to describe a woman .

(Sunny from Taiwan)

I called someone a bitch once, when I was with a bunch of girls at school - years ago - and they looked so shocked. I didn't know what it meant, so I looked it up in the dictionary and when I saw it meant a female dog, I wondered why they were so horrified. It didn't seem that bad a thing to call someone.

(Joyce)

# "You fucking bitch - I hope you realise you've probably ruined my career!"

(Scottish actor to the author in circa 1980 - when she was nine months pregnant . . . and in the pub! - after she had written a humorous diary piece for a Glasgow newspaper poking fun at the fact that the actor in question - who went on to become very successful - had been starring simultaniously in two alcohol ads: one for Tennents lager, the other for an alcohol awareness campaign, urging people to not overdrink.)

**First woman:** *"I never swear."*

**Second woman:** *"Yes you do - whenever you mention your ex-husband's new wife, you always refer to her as "THAT BITCH!" instead of using her actual name."*

I can tell you how to say *"what the fuck"* in eggy language: it's *"wheggat thegge fegguck"*.

(Tommy)

## About Deedee Cuddihy

Deedee Cuddihy is a journalist who was born and brought up in New York but has lived in Glasgow since the "Big Storm" of 1967 (which she slept through). Or was it 1968? After finishing art school in Glasgow, she realised being an artist would be too difficult - and being an art teacher would be even more difficult. So she became a journalist and has been one ever since. She is married to a Scotsman and has two grown up children - plus four granddaughters. "The Wee Guide to Scottish Swearing" is the 15th in her Funny Scottish Books series, the other titles including the best-selling "I Love Irn-Bru", "Only in Dundee" and "The Wee Guide to Scottish Women". She swears a lot (just ask her family).